Ten in the Meadow

For Finn Eric
J. B.

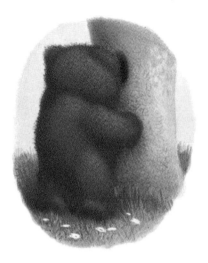

ISBN-13: 978-0-545-01691-9
ISBN-10: 0-545-01691-6

12 11 10 9 8 7 6 5 4   7 8 9 10 11 12/0

Printed in the U.S.A.   40

First Scholastic printing, March 2007

Illustrations created in acrylics and colored pencil.

Ten in the Meadow

John Butler

SCHOLASTIC INC.

New York Toronto London Auckland Sydney
Mexico City New Delhi Hong Kong Buenos Aires

Round and round the meadow,
Running here and there.

Ten little friends play hide-and-seek!

"Quickly, hide from Bear!"

Round and
round the daisies,
Bear shouts, "Here I come!"

He's searching . . .

he's looking . . .

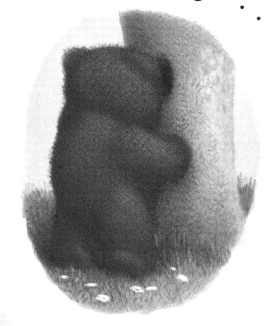

Here, he's found someone!

Round and round the foxgloves,

The two friends take a look.

Among the flowers,
under leaves,

They peek in
every nook.

"Found you, Porcupine!"

"Found you, Mole!"

Round and
round the bluebells,
The friends join in the race.

Looking here . . .

looking there . . .

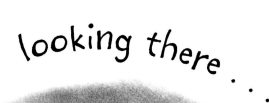

They've found a hiding place!

"Found you, Badger!"
"Found you, Fox!"

Little paws and bushy tails . . .

Who is up the tree?

"Found you, Squirrel!"
"Found you, Raccoon!"

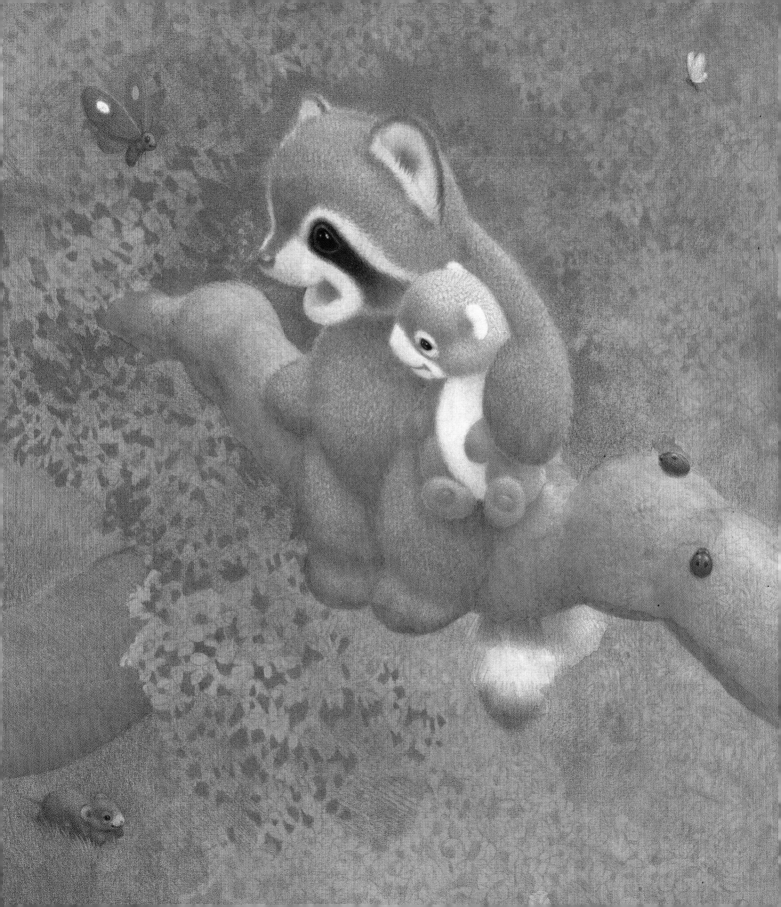

Who's that under the lily pads?
Shall we take a look?

Round and round the rushes,
By the trickling brook.

Round and round the clover,
The sun is sinking low.
Rabbit says, "Now, where is Mouse?
Does anybody know?"

"Where are you, Mouse?"

Round and round the willow,

Where can Mousey be?

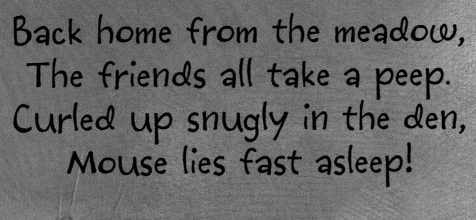

Back home from the meadow,
The friends all take a peep.
Curled up snugly in the den,
Mouse lies fast asleep!

"Shh, sleepy-time, everyone . . . "

Ten friends asleep together,
Below the crescent moon.
They dream about tomorrow's fun,
And games they'll all play soon.

Good night! Sleep tight!